APOSTOLIC FATHERS

DIDACHE

THE TEACHING OF THE TWELVE APOSTLES

(Bilingual English-Greek Edition)

Translation by Charles H. Hoole

Dear Reader,

If you have enjoyed the book and would like to support our publishing project, please consider providing a review about our product.

Very grateful.

Cover: *The Baptism of Jesus Christ*
(Arian Baptistery, Ravenna.)
(Based in the work of Peter Milošević)

INDEX

Introduction

Didache

INTRODUCTION

Time of Composition

The Didache has the marks of the highest antiquity and is one of the oldest, if not the very oldest, of the post-Apostolic writings. There is nothing in it which could not have been written between A.D. 70 and 100.

This is evident, negatively, from the absence of allusion to facts, movements, customs and institutions known throughout Christendom from the middle or beginning of the second century. No mention is made of a New Testament canon, or any book except "the Gospel;" there is no trace of a baptismal creed, or church festival (as Easter), or formulated dogma, or specific heresy, either Ebionism or Gnosticism, which were already rampant in the age of Trajan and Hadrian. The Didache is entirely uncontroversial.

Still more conclusive are the positive indications of antiquity. The *Didache* presents Christian teaching and Christian institutions in primitive, childlike simplicity. The Church appears in a state of orphanage, immediately after the death of its founders. Apostles still continue, but are of a lower grade and as it were dying out. The Prophets are the chief teachers and not yet superseded by the Bishops. Nor had the Presbyters taken the place of the primitive Bishops, but both are still identical. Of the supernatural gifts prophecy was flourishing, but the glossolalia and the power of miracles had disappeared. The Agape and the Eucharist are one feast; while from the beginning of the second century they were separated. There is no class distinction of clergy and laity, no mention of ordination, of three orders, of sacerdotal functions. Only two sacraments are mentioned. Discretionary freedom is allowed in the mode of administering Baptism, and room is left for the extemporaneous exercise of the gift of prayer in public worship, which had not yet assumed a settled order. No reading of Scripture lessons is even mentioned.

The eucharistic thanksgivings are much shorter and simpler than those in the ancient liturgies. The sixteenth chapter moves in the eschatological atmosphere of the Synoptical Gospels; and the whole book reflects the Jewish Christian stage of the Church in the land of its birth under the living power of the one Gospel of the Lord.

The antiquity is confirmed by the close affinity of the style and vocabulary to the writings of the New Testament, as distinct both from classical and from patristic Greek.

Let us reason back from the end of the second century when it was certainly known and used.

The *Didache* is older than Clement of Alexandria, c. 200, who already quoted it as "Scripture," regarding it as semi-Apostolic and semi-inspired. It cannot have been a new book then to be so highly esteemed.

It is older than Irenaeus, c. 180, and Justin Martyr, c. 140, who opposed the full-grown Gnostic heresy, and present a more advanced state of doctrinal development and ecclesiastical organization.

It is older than the *Epistle of Barnabas*, which was certainly written before 120, probably before 100; for Barnabas presents in the last chapters (which are wanting in the Latin version) a verbose and confused expansion of the first chapters of the *Didache* or some other similar document; while the *Didache* has all the marks of originality: brevity, simplicity and uniformity of style.

It is older than the *Shepherd of Hermas*, whether composed under Bishop Pius of Rome, 139-154, or much earlier at the time of Presbyter-Bishop Clement, 92-100: for in its brief parallel sections, Hermas is likewise an enlargement of the simpler statements of the Didache.

It is older than the oldest recension of the Ignatian Epistles, which dates from the first quarter of the second century: for Ignatius enforces with great earnestness the Episcopal office as a distinct order of the ministry superior to the Presbyterate, and opposes Gnostic docetism; while the *Didache* still identifies the Episcopate with the Presbyterate, and specifies no heresy.

This would bring us to the threshold of the Apostolic century.

Yet we cannot well go far back of the year 100. For the *Didache* in the eschatological chapter, makes no allusion to the destruction of Jerusalem as an impending event. And it is not likely that any writer should have undertaken to give a summary of the "Teaching of the Twelve Apostles," while one or more of them were still alive. James, Peter, and Paul, it is true, had suffered martyrdom before the destruction of Jerusalem; but John lived to the reign of Trajan, which began A.D. 98.

We may therefore assign the Didache with some confidence to the closing years of the first century, say between A.D. 90 and 100.

In the Jerusalem MS. our document follows the Clementine Epistles and precedes the Ignatian Epistles. This nearly indicates, whether intentionally or not, the probable date of its composition.

The views of scholars still vary considerably, but seem to incline with increasing unanimity to a very early date. Bryennios, on account of the supposed priority of Barnabas and Hermas, puts the *Didache* down to between A.D. 120-160; Harnack, for the same reason, to 120-165; Hilgenfeld and Bouet-Maury, who find in it anti-Montanistic features, assign its present shape to 160-190, and Krawutzcky traces it to Ebionitic origin at the close of the second century. But nearly all the other writers, especially the English and American scholars, favor an earlier date: Zahn between 80 and 120; Hitchcock and Brown between 100 and 120; Farrar, 100; Lightfoot, 80-100; Funk, Langen, Massebieau, Potwin, Sadler, De Romestin, Spence, assign it more or less confidently to the last quarter of the first century, Bestmann goes back even to 70-79.

Place of composition

The majority of scholars assign the Didache to Alexandria in Egypt a minority to Palestine or Syria.

Some city of Asia Minor, or of Greece, or even Rome, has also been conjectured, but without response.

The choice is between Egypt and Syria including Palestine.

For Alexandria speaks the fact that there the *Didache* seems to have been first known and quoted (by Clement of Alexandria), and used for catechetical instruction (according to

Athanasius). The kindred *Epistle of Barnabas* and the *Apostolical Church Order* are probably likewise of Egyptian origin.

But there is an insuperable objection to Egypt in the allusion, in one of the eucharistic prayers, to the broken bread which was "scattered (in grains) over the mountains". This is entirely inapplicable to the valley of the Nile and to the bare rocks on the border of the desert. Of less weight is the provision for exceptional baptism in *warm water* (Ch. VII. 2), which seems to point to a cold climate.

On the other hand, nothing can be said against, and much in favor of, Southern or Northern Syria as the fatherland of the *Didache*, provided we put its composition, as we must, before the Ignatian Epistles and the establishment of Episcopacy in Syria, as a separate order of the ministry.

Some considerations point strongly to Palestine and even to Jerusalem; the constant use of the Gospel of Matthew, which originated in that country; the affinity with the theology and practical genius of James, whose letter hails from the capital of the theocracy; and the approval of the community of goods (com p. 4: 8 with Acts, 4. 32), which seems to have been confined to that city The church of Jerusalem was indeed dispersed to Pella in the Decapolis during the Jewish war, but it was reconstructed afterwards and continued its existence down to the second and more complete destruction of the city under Hadrian, when its continuity was again interrupted.

The *Didache* is not unworthy of the mother church of Christendom, where once all the twelve Apostles lived and labored, where the first Christian Council was held, and where James the brother of the Lord spent his public life as the last connecting

11

link between the old and new dispensation and suffered martyrdom for his faith in Christ. That church was never much influenced by Paul's teaching and kept him at a respectful distance. This would well agree with the spirit of the *Didache*.

But nearly as much may be said for Antioch, the Northern capital of Syria, the mother church of Gentile Christianity, where the Christian name was first given to the disciples, where Jews and Gentiles first mingled into one community, and where the two nationalities first came into conflict with each other about the question of circumcision and the yoke of the ceremonial law. There, as well as in Jerusalem, all the conditions (except the community of goods) were given for such a Jewish-Christian Irenicum as the *Didache*. The book must have been well known in Syria, for there it was expanded and superseded by the Pseudo-Clementine Constitutions and Canons, which are certainly of Syrian origin.

Authorship

The author modestly concealed his name and gives no clue to his identification. But he was certainly a Jewish Christian, and probably a companion and pupil of the Apostles. He belongs to the school of Matthew and James; he emphasizes the legal and moral element in Christianity, but is fully pervaded at the same time by the spirit of charity, meekness, gentleness and generosity which animates the Gospel. He shows no influence of the ideas and doctrines of Paul, which had hardly reached the Jewish congregations, and never fully pervaded them. The few probable allusions to his Epistles refer to matters of common agreement. Yet he is no more opposed to Paul than either Matthew or

James. He may be said to be ante-Pauline (as to spirit, not as to time), but not anti-Pauline. He gives the teaching of the *Twelve Apostles* of Israel, but with no more intention of denying the authority of the Apostle of the Gentiles than the author of the Apocalypse when he speaks of the "Twelve Apostles" of the Lamb (21: 14). His style and phraseology are Hebraistic. He calls the Prophets "high priests." He refers to the first fruits of the produce, and to the Jewish fasts on Tuesday and Thursday. He calls Friday "Preparation Day." He is acquainted with the Old Testament and the Jewish Apocrypha (The Book of Ecclesiasticus and Tobit). He abstains from all polemics against the Jewish religion, and thereby differs strongly from the author of the *Epistle of Barnabas*. He enjoins the recital of the *Lord's Prayer* three times a day, in evident imitation of the Jewish hours of prayer. He abhors the eating of meat offered to the gods as a contamination with idolatry, and adheres to the compromise measures of the Council of Jerusalem, over which James presided. He even seems to recommend the bearing of the whole yoke of the law as a way to perfection, but he is far from requiring it or casting reflection upon the more liberal Gentile Christians. The whole sum of religion consists for him in perfect love to God and to our fellow-men as commanded in the Gospel, or in what James calls "the perfect law of liberty" (1: 25).

It does not follow, however, that the *Didache* was written exclusively for Jews; on the contrary, it is, according to the title, intended for "the nations" in the same sense in which the Gospel is to be preached to "all nations," according to the Lord's command in Matthew (28: 19).

Beyond this we cannot safely go. The real author will probably remain unknown as much as the author of the *Epistle to the*

Hebrews, which is of the order of Melchizedek, "without father, without mother, without genealogy, having neither beginning of days nor end of life."

In conclusion, we mention two conjectures as to authorship, which have been proposed by the most recent writers on the *Didache* and which are about equally ingenious and plausible, but alike destitute of solid foundation.

Canon Spence assigns the authorship to Bishop Symeon of Jerusalem, the son of Cleopas, the nephew of Joseph and cousin of our Lord, who, according to Hegesippus in Eusebius, succeeded James the Less after his martyrdom, and ruled the Pella community in the Decapolis from about 69 to 106. He wrote the Didache between 80 and 90 as a manual for the instruction of the surrounding heathens.

Dr. Bestmann goes further back, to the momentous collision between Paul and Peter at Antioch before the church, and the reaction of Jewish conservatism under the lead of James of Jerusalem. Soon after the destruction of the city the Didache was issued as a Manifesto and Ultimatum of the Jewish section of the Antiochian Church, but was rejected by the Gentile portion, which issued the *Epistle of Barnabas* as a counter-Manifesto.

This Epistle shows that God had already, through the Prophets, and then through Christ, abolished the law as an outward ordinance, that the unbelieving Jews have no claim to the Old Testament, and that it is only an allegory of Christianity. The opposition, however, was softened by the *Appendix of the Two Ways*, which was added to Barnabas for the purpose of exhibiting the harmony of the Jewish and Hellenic sections of the

Church in the fundamental moral principles and practices of Christianity.

Lessons of the Didache

The Didache has no more authority than any other post-Apostolic writing. The truths it contains and the duties it enjoins are independently known to us from the Scriptures, and are binding upon us as revelations of Christ and his Apostles. It is not free from superstitious notions and mechanical practices which are foreign to Apostolic wisdom and freedom. Its value is historical and historical only, but this is very considerable, and exceeds that of any known post-Apostolic document. It touches upon a greater variety of topics than any of the Apostolic Fathers, so-called, and gives us a clearer insight into the condition of the Church in the transition period between A. D. 70 and 150.

The following is a summary of the lessons of the Didache as regards the state of Christianity in that part of the East here the author resided.

1. Catechetical instruction was required as a preparation for church membership.

2. That instruction was chiefly moral and practical, and based upon the Decalogue and the Sermon on the Mount. No doubt, it included also the main facts in the life of Christ; for the document assumes throughout faith in Christ as our Lord and Savior, and repeatedly refers to his Gospel.

3. The moral code was of the highest order, far above that of any other religion or school of philosophy. It was summed up

in the two royal commandments of supreme love to God and love to our neighbor, as explained by the teaching and example of Christ. It emphasized purity, gentleness, humility, and charity. The superior morality of Christianity in theory and practice carried in it the guarantee of its ultimate victory.

4 Baptism was the rite of initiation into church membership, and was usually administered by trine immersion in a river (in imitation of Christ's Baptism in the Jordan), but with a margin for freedom as to the quality of water and the mode of its application; and threefold aspersion of the head was allowed as legitimate Baptism in case of scarcity of the element. Fasting before the act was required, but no oil, salt, or exorcism, or any other material or ceremony is mentioned.

5. The Eucharist was celebrated every Lord's Day in connection with the Agape (as at Corinth in the time of Paul), and consisted of a fraternal meal, thanksgivings and free prayers for the temporal and spiritual mercies of God in Christ. It was regarded as the Christian sacrifice of thanksgiving to be offered everywhere and to the end of time, according to the prophecy of Malachi.

6. There were no other sacraments but these two. At least none is even hinted at.

7. The *Lord's Prayer* with the doxology was repeated three times a day. This, together with the Eucharistic prayers, constituted the primitive liturgy; but freedom was given to the Prophets to pray from the heart in public worship.

8. The first day of the week was celebrated as the Lord's Day (in commemoration of his resurrection), by public worship

and the Eucharist; and Wednesday and Friday were observed as days of fasting (in commemoration of the Passion).

9. The Church at large was extended and governed by travelling Apostles (or Evangelists), who carried the Gospel to unknown parts, and by Prophets either itinerant or stationary, who instructed, comforted and revived the converts; while the local congregations were governed by Bishops (or Presbyters) and Deacons, elected and supported by the Christian people.

10. Most of the books of the New Testament, especially the Gospel of Matthew, were more or less known, and their authority recognized, but there was as yet no settled canon of the Scriptures, and the quotations and reminiscences were more from living teaching than from written books.

11. Outside of the Gospel tradition nothing of any importance was known concerning Christ and the Apostles. The *Didache* mentions only one extra-canonical sentence, of uncertain authorship (1: 6.), possibly a reported saying of our Lord, but it adds nothing of consequence to the twenty-three sentences which tradition ascribes to Him. As Bishop Lightfoot says, "All the evangelical matter, so far as we can trace it, is found within the four corners of our canonical Gospels."

12. Christians are to live in prayerful expectation of the glorious coming of Christ and to keep) themselves always in readiness for it.

Philip Schaff

17

CHAPTER I
THE TWO WAYS. THE WAY OF LIFE

1:1 There are two paths, one of life and one of death[1], and the difference is great between the two paths.

1:1 Ὁδοὶ δύο εἰσί, μία τῆς ζωῆς καὶ μία τοῦ θανάτου, διαφορὰ δὲ πολλὴ μεταξὺ τῶν δύο ὁδῶν.

1:2 Now the path of life is this -- first, thou shalt love the God who made thee, thy neighbor as thyself[2], and all things that thou wouldest not should be done unto thee, do not thou unto another[3].

1:2 Ἡ μὲν οὖν τῆς ζωῆς ἐστιν αὕτη· πρῶτον ἀγαπησεις τὸν θεὸν τὸν ποιήσαντά σε, δεύτερον τὸν πλησίον σου ὡς σεαυτόν· πάντα δὲ ὅσα ἐὰν θελήσῃς μὴ γίνεσθαί σοι, καὶ σὺ ἄλλῳ μὴ ποίει.

1:3 And the doctrine of these maxims is as follows. Bless them that curse you, and pray for your enemies[4]. Fast on behalf of those that persecute you; for what thank is there if ye love them that love you? Do not even the Gentiles do the same?[5] But do ye love them that hate you, and ye will not have an enemy.

1:3 Τούτων δὲ τῶν λόγων ἡ διδαχή ἐστιν αὕτη· εὐλογεῖτε τοὺς καταρωμένους ὑμῖν καὶ προσεύχεσθε ὑπὲρ τῶν ἐχθρῶν ὑμῶν, νηστεύετε δὲ ὑπὲρ τῶν διωκότων ὑμᾶς· ποία γὰρ χάρις, ἐὰν

---

[1] Jer. 31: 8; Deut. 30: 15, 16, 19; Matt. 7: 13, 14.
[2] Matt. 22: 37, 39.
[3] Matt. 7: 12; Luke 6: 31.
[4] Matt. 5: 48; Luke. 6: 27, 28.
[5] Matt. 5: 46; Luke. 6: 32.

ἀγαπᾶτε τοὺς ἀγαπῶντας ὑμᾶς; οὐχὶ καὶ τὰ ἔθνη τὸ αὐτὸ ποιοῦσιν; ὑμεῖς δὲ ἀγαπᾶτε τοὺς μισοῦντας ὑμᾶς, καὶ οὐχ ἕξετε ἐχτρόν.

1:4 Abstain from fleshly and worldly[6] lusts. If anyone give thee a blow on thy right cheek, turn unto him the other also[7], and thou shalt be perfect[8]; if any one compel thee to go a mile, go with him two;[9] if a man take away thy cloak, give him thy coat also[10]; if a man take from thee what is thine, ask not for it again,[11] for neither art thou able to do so.

1:4 ἀπέχου τῶν σαρκικῶν καὶ σωματικῶν ἐπιθυμιῶν· ἐὰν τίς σοι δῷ ῥάπισμα εἰς τὴν δεξιὰν σιαγόνα, στέψον αὐτῷ καὶ τὴν ἄλλην, καὶ ἔσῃ τέλειος· ἐὰν ἀγγαρεύσῃ σέ τις μίλιον ἕν, ὕπαγε μετ' αυτοῦ δύο· ἐὰν ἄρῃ τις τὸ ἱμάτιόν σου, δὸς αὐτῷ καὶ τὸν χιτῶνα· ἐὰν λάβῃ τις ἀπὸ σοῦ τὸ σόν, μὴ ἀπαίτει· οὐδὲ γὰρ δύνασαι.

1:5 Give to everyone that asks of thee, and ask not again;[12] for the Father wishes that from his own gifts there should be given to all. Blessed is he who giveth according to the commandment, for he is free from guilt; but woe unto him that receives. For if a man receive being in need, he shall be free from guilt; but he who receives when not in need, shall pay a penalty as to why he received and for what purpose; and when he is in tribulation he shall be examined concerning the

---

[6] 1 Pet. 2: 11.
[7] Matt. 5: 39; Luke 6:29
[8] Matt. 5: 48; 19: 21.
[9] Matt. 5: 41.
[10] Matt. 5: 40; Luke 6: 29.
[11] Luke 5: 30; Matt. 5: 42.
[12] Luke 6: 30.

things that he has done, and shall not depart thence until he has paid the last farthing.[13]

1:5 παντὶ τῷ αἰτοῦντί σε δίδου καὶ μὴ ἀπαίτει· πᾶσι γὰρ θέλει δίδοσθαι ὁ πατὴρ ἐκ τῶν ἰδίων χαρισμάτων. μακάριος ὁ διδοὺς κατὰ τὴν ἐντολήν· ἀθῷος γάρ ἐστιν. οὐαὶ τῷ λαμβάνοντι· εἰ μὲν γὰρ γὰρ χρείαν ἔχων λαμβάνει τις, ἀθῷος ἔσται· ὁ δὲ μὴ χρείαν ἔχων δώσει δίκην, ἱνατί ἔλαβε καὶ εἰς τί· ἐν συνοχῇ δὲ γενόμενος ἐξετασθήσεται περὶ ὧν ἔπραξε, καὶ οὐκ ἐξελεύσεται ἐκεῖθεν, μέχρις οὗ ἀποδῷ τὸν ἔσχατον κοδράντην.

1:6 For of a truth it has been said on these matters, let thy almsgiving abide in thy hands until thou knowest to whom thou hast given.

1:6 ἀλλὰ καὶ περὶ τούτου δὲ εἴρηται· Ἱδρωσάτω ἡ ἐλεημοσύνη σου εἰς τὰς χεῖράς σου, μέχρις ἂν γνῷς τίνι δῷς.

CHAPTER II
THE SECOND GREAT COMMANDMENT
WARNING AGAINST GROSS SINS

2:1 But the second commandment of the teaching is this.

2:1 Δευτέρα δὲ ἐντολὴ τῆς διδαχῆς·

2:2 Thou shalt not kill;[14] thou shalt not commit adultery;[15] thou shalt not corrupt youth; thou shalt not commit

---

[13] Matt. 5: 26.
[14] Ex. 20: 13.
[15] Ex. 20: 14.

fornication; thou shalt not steal;[16] thou shalt not use sooth-saying; thou shalt not practise sorcery; thou shalt not kill a child by abortion, neither shalt thou slay it when born; thou shalt not covet the goods of thy neighbour;[17]

2:2 οὐ φονεύσεις, οὐ μοιχεύσεις, οὐ παιδοφθορήσεις, οὐ πορνεύσεις, οὐ κλέψεις, οὐ μαγεύσεις, οὐ φαρμακεύσεις, οὐ φονεύσεις τέκνον ἐν φθορᾷ, οὐδὲ γεννηθὲν ἀποκτενεῖς, οὐκ ἐπιθυμήσεις τὰ τοῦ πλησίον.

2:3 thou shalt not commit perjury;[18] thou shalt not bear false witness;[19] thou shalt not speak evil; thou shalt not bear malice;

2:3 οὐκ ἐπιορκήσεις, οὐ ψευδομαρτυρήσεις, οὐ κακολογήσεις, οὐ μνησικακήσεις.

2:4 thou shalt not be double-minded or double-tongued, for to be double tongued is the snare of death.

2:4 οὐκ ἔσῃ διγνώμων οὐδὲ δίγλωσσος· παγὶς γὰρ θανάτου ἡ διγλωσσία.

2:5 Thy speech shall not be false or empty, but concerned with action.

2:5 οὐκ ἔσται ὁ λόγος σου ψευδής, οὐ κενός, ἀλλὰ μεμεστωμένος πράξει.

---

[16] Ex. 20: 15.
[17] Ex. 20: 17.
[18] Matt. 5: 33
[19] Ex. 20: 16

2:6 Thou shalt not be covetous, or rapacious, or hypocritical, or malicious, or proud; thou shalt not take up an evil design against thy neighbour;

2:6 οὐκ ἔσῃ πλεονέκτης οὐδὲ ἅρπαξ οὐδὲ ὑποκριτὴς οὐδὲ κακοήθης οὐδὲ ὑπερήφανος. οὐ λήψῃ βουλὴν πονηρὰν κατὰ τοῦ πλησίον σου.

2:7 thou shalt not hate any man, but some thou shalt confute,[20] concerning some thou shalt pray, and some thou shalt love beyond thine own soul.

2:7 οὐ μισήσεις πάντα ἄνθρώπον, ἀλλὰ οὓς μὲν ἐλέγξεις, περὶ δὲ ὧν προσεύξῃ, οὓς δὲ ἀγαπήσεις ὑπὲρ τὴν ψυχήν σου.

CHAPTER III
WARNING AGAINST LIGHTER SINS

3:1 My child, fly from everything that is evil, and from everything that is like to it.[21]

3.1 Τέκνον μου, φεῦγε ἀπὸ παντὸς πονηροῦ καὶ ἀπὸ παντὸς ὁμοίου αὐτου.

3:2 Be not wrathful, for wrath leads unto slaughter; be not jealous, or contentious, or quarrelsome, for from all these things slaughter ensues.

3.2 μὴ γίνου ὀργίλος, ὁδηγεῖ γὰρ ἡ ὀργὴ πρὸς τὸν φόνον, μηδὲ ζηλωτὴς μηδὲ ἐπιστικὸς μηδὲ θυμικός· ἐκ γὰρ τούτων ἁπάντων φόνοι γεννῶνται.

---

[20] Lev. 19: 17.
[21] 1 Thess. 5: 22

3:3 My child, be not lustful, for lust leads unto fornication; be not a filthy talker; be not a lifter up of the eye, for from all these things come adulteries.

3.3. τέκνον μου, μὴ γίνου ἐπιθυμητής, ὁδηγεῖ γὰρ ἡ ἐπιθυμία πρὸς τὴν πορνείαν, μηδὲ αἰσχχρολόγος μηδὲ ὑψηλόφθαλμος· ἐκ γὰρ τούτων ἁπαντων μοιχεῖαι γεννῶνται.

3:4 My child, be not an observer of omens, since it leads to idolatry, nor a user of spells, nor an astrologer, nor a travelling purifier, nor wish to see these things, for from all these things idolatry arises.

3.4 τέκνον μου, μὴ γίνου οἰωνοσκόπος, ἐπειδὴ ὁδηγεῖ εἰς τὴν εἰδωλολοατρίαν, μηδὲ ἐπαοιδὸς μηδὲ μαθηματικὸς μηδὲ περικαθαθαίρων, μηδὲ θέλε αὐτὰ βλέπειν· ἐκ γὰρ τούτων ἁπάντων εἰδωλολατρία γεννᾶται.

3:5 My child, be not a liar, for lying leads unto theft; be not covetous or conceited, for from all these things thefts arise.

3:5 τέκνον μου, μὴ γίνου ψεύστης, ἐπειδὴ ὁδηγεῖ τὸ ψεῦσμα εἰς τὴν κλοπήν, μηδὲ φιλάργυρος μηδὲ κενόδοξος· ἐκ γὰρ τούτων ἁπάντων κλοπαὶ γεννῶνται.

3:6 My child, be not a murmurer, since it leads unto blasphemy; be not self-willed or evil-minded, for from all these things blasphemies are produced;

3:6 τέκνον μου, μὴ γίνου γόγγυσος, ἐπειδὴ ὁδηγεῖ εἰς τὴν βλασφημίαν, μηδὲ αὐθάδης μηδὲ πονηρόφρων· ἐκ γὰρ τούτων ἁπάντων βλασφημίαι γεννῶνται.

3:7 but be thou meek, for the meek shall inherit the earth;[22]

3:7 ἴσθι δὲ πραΰς, ἐπεὶ οἱ πραεῖς κληρονομήσουσι τὴν γῆν.

3:8 be thou longsuffering, and compassionate, and harmless, and peaceable, and good, and fearing always the words that thou hast heard.[23]

3:8 γίνου μακρόθυμος καὶ ἐλεήμων καὶ ἄκακος καὶ ἡσύχιος καὶ ἀγαθὸς καὶ τρέμων τοὺς λόγους διὰ παντός, οὓς ἤκουσας.

3:9 Thou shalt not exalt thyself, neither shalt thou put boldness into thy soul. Thy soul shall not be joined unto the lofty, but thou shalt walk with the just and humble.[24]

3:9 οὐχ ὑψώσεις σεαυτὸν οὐδὲ δώσεις τῇ ψυχῇ σου θράσος. οὐ κολληθήσεται ἡ ψυχή σου μετὰ ὑψηλῶν, ἀλλὰ μετὰ δικαίων καὶ ταπεινῶν ἀναστραφήσῃ.

3:10 Accept the things that happen to thee as good, knowing that without God nothing happens.

3:10 τὰ συμβαίνοντά σοι ἐνεργήματα ὡς ἀγαθὰ προσδέξῃ, εἰδὼς ὅτι ἄτερ θεοῦ οὐδὲν γίνεται.

---

[22] Matt. 5: 5.
[23] Isa. 66. 2: 5.
[24] Rom. 12: 16.

CHAPTER IV
SUNDRY WARNINGS AND EXHORTATIONS

4:1 My child, thou shalt remember both night and day him that speaks unto thee the Word of God;[25] thou shalt honour him as thou dost the Lord, for where the teaching of the Lord is given, there is the Lord;

4:1 Τέκνον μου, τοῦ λαλοῦντός σοι τὸν λόγον τοῦ θεοῦ μνησθήσῃ νυκτὸς καὶ ἡμέρας, τιμήσεις δὲ αὐτὸν ὡς κύριον· ὅθεν γὰρ ἡ κυριότης λαλεῖται, ἐκεῖ κύριός ἐστιν.

4:2 thou shalt seek out day by day the favour of the saints, that thou mayest rest in their words;

4:2 ἐκζητήσεις δὲ καθ᾽ ἡμέραν τὰ πρόσωπα τῶν ἁγίων, ἵνα ἐπαναπαῇς τοῖς λόγοις αὐτῶν.

4:3 thou shalt not desire schism, but shalt set at peace them that contend; thou shalt judge righteously; thou shalt not accept the person of any one to convict him of transgression;

4:3 οὐ ποθήσεις σχίσμα, εἰρηνεύσεις δὲ μαχομένους· κρινεῖς δικαίως, οὐ λήψῃ πρόσωπον ἐλέγξαι ἐπὶ παραπτώμασιν.

4:4 thou shalt not doubt whether a thing shall be or not.[26]

4:4 οὐ διψυχήσεις, πότερον ἔσται ἢ οὔ.

4:5 Be not a stretcher out of thy hand to receive, and a drawer of it back in giving.[27]

---

[25] Heb. 13: 7.
[26] Sir. 1: 28; James 1: 8; 4: 8.
[27] Ecclus. 4: 31.

4:5 Μὴ γίνου πρὸς μὲν τὸ λαβεῖν ἐκτείνων τὰς χεῖρας, πρὸς δὲ τὸ δοῦναι συσπῶν.

4:6 If thou hast, give by means of thy hands a redemption for thy sins.[28]

4:6 ἐὰν ἔχῃς διὰ τῶν χειρῶν σου, δώσεις λύτρωσιν ἁμαρτιῶν σου.

4:7 Thou shalt not doubt to give, neither shalt thou murmur when giving; for thou shouldest know who is the fair recompenser of the reward.

4:7 οὐ διστάσεις δοῦναι οὐδὲ διδοὺς γογγύσεις· γνώσῃ γάρ, τίς ἐστιν ὁ τοῦ μισθοῦ καλὸς ἀνταποδότης.

4:8 Thou shalt not turn away from him that is in need, but shalt share with thy brother in all things, and shalt not say that things are thine own;[29] **for if ye are partners in what is immortal, how much more in what is mortal?**[30]

4:8 οὐκ ἀποστραφήσῃ τὸν ἐνδεόμενον, συγκοινωνήσεις δὲ πάντα τῷ ἀδελφῷ σου καὶ οὐκ ἐρεῖς ἴδια εἶναι· εἰ γὰρ ἐν τῷ ἀθανάτῳ κοινωνοί ἐστε, πόσῳ μᾶλλον ἐν τοῖς θνητοῖς;

4:9 Thou shalt not remove thine heart from thy son or from thy daughter, but from their youth shalt teach them the fear of God.

---

[28] Dan. 4: 27; Tobit 4: 10, 11.
[29] Acts. 4: 32.
[30] Rom. 15: 27.

4:9 Οὐκ ἀρεῖς τὴν χεῖρα σου ἀπὸ τοῦ υἱοῦ σου ἢ ἀπὸ τῆς θυγατρός σου, ἀλλὰ ἀπὸ νεότητος διδάξεις τὸν φόβον τοῦ θεοῦ.

4:10 Thou shalt not command with bitterness thy servant or thy handmaid, who hope in the same God as thyself, lest they fear not in consequence the God who is over both;[31] for he comes not to call with respect of persons, but those whom the Spirit has prepared.

4:10 οὐκ ἐπιτάξεις δούλῳ σου ἢ παιδίσκῃ, τοῖς ἐπὶ τὸν αὐτὸν θεὸν ἐλπίζουσιν, ἐν πικρίᾳ σου, μήποτε οὐ μὴ φοβηθήσονται τὸν ἐπ' ἀμφοτέροις θεόν· οὐ γὰρ ἔρχεται κατὰ πρόσωπον καλέσαι, ἀλλ' ἐφ' οὓς τὸ πνεῦμα ἡτοίμασεν.

4:11 And do ye servants submit yourselves to your masters with reverence and fear, as being the type of God.[32]

4:11 ὑμεῖς δὲ οἱ δοῦλοι ὑποταγήσεσθε τοῖς κυρίοις ὑμῶν ὡς τύπτῳ θεοῦ ἐν αἰσχύνῃ καὶ φόβῳ.

4:12 Thou shalt hate all hypocrisy and everything that is not pleasing to God;

4:12 Μισήσεις πᾶσαν ὑπόκρισιν καὶ πᾶν ὃ μὴ ἀρεστὸν τῷ κυρίῳ.

4:13 thou shalt not abandon the commandments of the Lord, but shalt guard that which thou hast received, neither adding thereto nor taking therefrom;[33]

---

[31] Eph. 6: 9; Col. 4: 1.
[32] Eph. 6: 5; Col. 3: 22.
[33] Deut. 12: 32.

4:13 οὐ μὴ ἐγκαταλίπῃς ἐντολὰς κυρίου, φυλάξεις δὲ ἃ παρέλαβες, μήτε προστιθεὶς μήτε ἀφαιρῶν.

4:14 thou shalt confess thy transgressions in the Church,[34] and shalt not come unto prayer with an evil conscience. This is the path of life.

4:14 ἐν ἐκκλησίᾳ ἐξομολογήσῃ τὰ παραπτώματά σου, καὶ οὐ προσελεύσῃ ἐπὶ προσευχήν σου ἐν συνειδήσει πονηρᾷ· αὕτη ἐστὶν ἡ ὁδὸς τῆς ζωῆς.

CHAPTER V
THE WAY OF DEATH

5:1 But the path of death is this. First of all, it is evil, and full of cursing; there are found murders, adulteries, lusts, fornication, thefts, idolatries, soothsaying, sorceries, robberies, false witnessings, hypocrisies, double-mindedness, craft, pride, malice, self-will, covetousness, filthy talking, jealousy, audacity, pride, arrogance;

5:1 Ἡ δὲ τοῦ θανάτου ὁδός ἐστιν αὕτη· πρῶτον πάντων πονηρά ἐστι καὶ κατάρας μεστή· φόνοι, μοιχεῖαι, ἐπιθυμίαι, προνεῖαι, κλοπαί, εἰδωλολατρίαι, μαγεῖαι, φαρμακίαι, ἁρπαγαί, ψευδομαρτυρίαι, ὑποκρίσεις, διπλοκαρδία, δόλος, ὑπερηφανία, κακία, αὐθάδεια, πλεονεξία, αἰσχρολογία, ζηλοτυπία, θρασύτης, ὕψος, ἀλαζονεία.

---

[34] James 5: 16.

5:2 there are they who persecute the good – lovers of a lie,[35] not knowing the reward of righteousness, not cleaving to the good nor to righteous judgment, watching not for the good but for the bad, from whom meekness and patience are afar off, loving things that are vain, following after recompense, having no compassion on the needy, nor labouring for him that is in trouble, not knowing him that made them, murderers of children, corrupters of the image of God, who turn away from him that is in need, who oppress him that is in trouble, unjust judges of the poor, erring in all things. From all these, children, may ye be delivered.

5:2 διῶκται ἀγαθῶν, μισοῦντες ἀλήθειαν, ἀγαπῶντες ψεῦδος, οὐ γινώσκοντες μισθὸν δικαιοσύνης, οὐ κολλώμενοι ἀγαθῷ οὐδὲ κρίσει δικαίᾳ ἀγρυπνοῦντες οὐκ εἰς τὸ ἀγαθόν, ἀλλ' εἰς τὸ πονηρόν· ὧν μακρὰν πραΰτης καὶ ὑπομονή, μάταια ἀγαπῶντες, διώκοντες ἀνταπόδομα, οὐκ ἐλεοῦντες πτωχόν, οὐ πονοῦντες ἐπὶ καταπονουμένῳ, οὐ γινώσκοντες τὸν ποιήσαντα αὐτούς, φονεῖς τέκνων, φθορεῖς πλάσματος θεοῦ, ἀποστρεφόμενοι τὸν ἐνδεόμενον, καταπονοῦντες τὸν θλιβόμενον, πλουσίων παράκλητοι, πενήτων ἄνομοι κριταί, πανθαμάρτητοι· ῥυσθείητε, τέκνα, ἀπὸ τούτων ἁπάντων.

CHAPTER VI
WARNING AGAINST FALSE TEACHERS
AND THE WORSHIP OF IDOLS

6:1 See that no one make thee to err from this path of doctrine, since he who does so teaches thee apart from God.

---

[35] Rev. 22: 15.

6:1 Ὅρα, μὴ τίς σε πλανήσῃ ἀπὸ ταύτης τῆς ὁδοῦ τῆς διδαχῆς, ἐπεὶ παρεκτὸς θεοῦ σε διδάσκει.

6:2 If thou art able to bear the whole yoke of the Lord, thou wilt be perfect; but if thou art not able, what thou art able, that do.
6:2 εἰ μὲν γὰρ δύνασαι βαστάσαι ὅλον τὸν ζυγὸν τοῦ κυρίου, τέλειος ἔσῃ· εἰ δ' οὐ δύνασαι, ὃ δύνῃ, τοῦτο ποίει.

6:3 But concerning meat, bear that which thou art able to do. But keep with care from things sacrificed to idols, for it is the worship of the infernal deities.
6:3 περὶ δὲ τῆς βρώσεως, ὃ δύνασαι βάστασον· ἀπὸ δὲ τοῦ εἰδωλοθύτου λίαν πρόσεχε· λατρεία γάρ ἐστι θεῶν νεκρῶν.

CHAPTER VII
BAPTISM

7:1 But concerning baptism, thus baptize ye: having first recited all these precepts, baptize in the name of the Father, and of the Son, and of the Holy Spirit, in running water;
7:1 Περὶ δὲ τοῦ βαπτίσματος, οὕτω βαπτίσατε· ταῦτα πάντα προειπόντες, βαπτίσατε εἰς τὸ ὄνομα τοῦ πατρὸς καὶ τοῦ υἱοῦ καὶ τοῦ ἁγίου πνεύματος ἐν ὕδατι ζῶντι.

7:2 but if thou hast not running water, baptize in some other water, and if thou canst not baptize in cold, in warm water;
7:2 ἐὰν δὲ μὴ ἔχῃς ὕδωρ ζῶν, εἰς ἄλλο ὕδωρ βάπτισον· εἰ δ' οὐ δύνασαι ἐν ψυχρῷ, ἐν θερμῷ.

7:3 but if thou hast neither, pour water three times on the head, in the name of the Father, and of the Son, and of the Holy Spirit.

7:3 ἐὰν δὲ ἀμφότερα μὴ ἔχῃς, ἔκχεον εἰς τὴν κεφαλὴν τρὶς ὕδωρ εἰς ὄνομα πατρὸς καὶ υἱοῦ καὶ ἁγίου πνεύματος.

7:4 But before the baptism, let him who baptizes and him who is baptized fast previously, and any others who may be able. And thou shalt command him who is baptized to fast one or two days before.

7:4 πρὸ δὲ τοῦ βαπτίσματος προνηστευσάτω ὁ βαπτίζων καὶ ὁ βαπτιζόμενος καὶ εἴ τινες ἄλλοι δύναται· κελεύεις δὲ νηστεῦσαι τὸν βαπτιζόμενον πρὸ μιᾶς ἢ δύο.

CHAPTER VIII
PRAYER AND FASTING

8:1 But as for your fasts, let them not be with the hypocrites,[36] for they fast on the second and fifth days of the week, but do ye fast on the fourth and sixth days.

8:1 Αἱ δὲ νηστεῖαι ὑμῶν μὴ ἔστωσαν μετὰ τῶν ὑποκριτῶν. νηστεύουσι γὰρ δευτέρᾳ σαββάτων καὶ πέμπτῃ· ὑμεῖς δὲ νηστεύσατε τετράδα καὶ παρασκευήν.

8:2 Neither pray ye as the hypocrites,[37] but as the Lord hath commanded in his gospel so pray ye: Our Father in heaven,

---

[36] Matt. 6: 16.
[37] Matt. 6: 5.

hallowed be thy name. Thy kingdom come. Thy will be done as in heaven so on earth. Give us this day our daily bread. And forgive us our debt, as we also forgive our debtors. And lead us not into temptation, but deliver us from the evil: for thine is the power, and the glory, for ever.[38]

8:2 μηδὲ προσεύχεσθε ὡς οἱ ὑποκριταί, ἀλλ' ὡς ἐκέλευσεν ὁ κύριος ἐν τῷ εὐαγγελίῳ αὐτοῦ, οὕτω προσεύχεσθε· Πάτερ ἡμῶν ὁ ἐν τῷ οὐρανῷ, ἁγιασθήτω τὸ ὄνομά σου, ἐλθέτω ἡ βασιλεία σου, γενηθήτω τὸ θέλημά σου ὡς ἐν οὐρανῷ καὶ ἐπὶ γῆς· τὸν ἄρτον ἡμῶν τὸν ἐπιούσιον δὸς ἡμῖν σήμερον, καὶ ἄφες ἡμῖν τὴν ὀφειλη ὡς καὶ ἡμεῖς ἀφίεμεν τοῖς οφειλέταις ἡμῶν, καὶ μὴ εἰσενέγκης ἡμᾶς εἰς πειρασμόν, ἀλλὰ ῥῦσαι ἡμᾶς ἀπὸ τοῦ πονηροῦ· ὅτι σοῦ ἐστιν ἡ δύναμις καὶ ἡ δόξα εἰς τοὺς αἰῶνας.

8:3 Thrice a day pray ye in this fashion.

8:3 τρὶς τῆς ἡμέρας οὕτω προσεύχεσθε.

CHAPTER IX
THE AGAPE AND THE EUCHARIST

9:1 But concerning the Eucharist, after this fashion give ye thanks.

9:1 Περὶ δὲ τῆς εὐχαριστίας, οὕτως εὐχαριστήσατε·

9:2 First, concerning the cup. We thank thee, our Father, for the holy vine, David thy Son, which thou hast made

---

[38] Matt. 6: 9-13.

known unto us through Jesus Christ thy Son; to thee be the glory for ever.

9:2 πρῶτον περὶ τοῦ ποτηρίονυ Εὐχαριστοῦμεν σοι, πάτερ ἡμῶν, ὑπὲρ τῆς ἁγίας ἀμπέλου Δαυεὶδ τοῦ παιδός σου· σοὶ ἡ δόξα εἰς τοὺς αἰῶνας.

9:3 And concerning the broken bread. We thank thee, our Father, for the life and knowledge which thou hast made known unto us through Jesus thy Son; to thee be the glory for ever.

9:3 περὶ δὲ τοῦ κλάσματος· Εὐχαριστοῦμέν σοι, πάτερ ἡμῶν, ὑπὲρ τῆς ζωῆς καὶ γνώσεως, ἧς ἐγνώρισας ἡμῖν διὰ Ἰησοῦ τοῦ παιδός σου. σοὶ ἡ δόξα εἰς τοὺς αἰῶνας.

9:4 As this broken bread was once scattered on the mountains, and after it had been brought together became one, so may thy Church be gathered together from the ends of the earth unto thy kingdom; for thine is the glory, and the power, through Jesus Christ, for ever.

9:4 ὥσπερ ἦν τοῦτο τὸ κλάσμα διεσκορπισμένον ἐπάνω τῶν ὀρέων καὶ συναχθὲν ἐγένετο ἕν, οὕτω συναχθήτω σου ἡ ἐκκλησία ἀπὸ τῶν περάτων τῆς γῆς εἰς τὴν σὴν βασιλείαν. ὅτι σοῦ ἐστιν ἡ δόξα καὶ ἡ δύναμις διὰ Ἰησοῦ Χριστοῦ εἰς τοὺς αἰῶνας.

9:5 And let none eat or drink of your Eucharist but such as have been baptized into the name of the Lord, for of a truth the Lord has said concerning this, *Give not that which is holy unto dogs.*[39]

9:5 μηδεὶς δὲ φαγέτω μηδὲ πιέτω ἀπὸ τῆς εὐχαριστίας ὑμῶν, ἀλλ' οἱ βαπτισθέντες εἰς ὄνομα κυρίου· καὶ γὰρ περὶ τούτου εἴρηκεν ὁ κύριος· Μὴ δῶτε τὸ ἅγιον τοῖς κυσί.

CHAPTER X
POST-COMMUNION PRAYER

10:1 But after it has been completed, so pray ye.

10.1 Μετὰ δὲ τὸ ἐμπλησθῆναι οὕτως εὐχαριστήσατε·

10:2 We thank thee, holy Father, for thy holy name, which thou hast caused to dwell in our hearts, and for the knowledge and faith and immortality which thou hast made known unto us through Jesus thy Son; to thee be the glory for ever.

10:2 Εὐχαριστοῦμέν σοι, πάτερ ἅγιε, ὑπὲρ τοῦ ἁγίου ὀνόματός σου, οὗ κατεσκήνωσας ἐν ταῖς καρδίαις ἡμῶν, καὶ ὑπὲρ τῆς γνώσεως καὶ πίστεως καὶ ἀθανασίας, ἧς ἐγνώρισας ἡμῖν διὰ Ἰησοῦ τοῦ παιδός σου· σοὶ ἡ δόξα εἰς τοὺς αἰῶνας.

10:3 Thou, Almighty Master, didst create all things for the sake of thy name, and hast given both meat and drink, for men to enjoy, that we might give thanks unto thee, but to us thou hast given spiritual meat and drink, and life everlasting, through thy Son.

---

[39] Matt. 7: 6.

10:3 σύ, δέσποτα παντοκράτορ, ἔκτισας τὰ πάντα ἕνεκεν τοῦ ὀνόματός σου, τροφήν τε καὶ ποτὸν ἔδωκας τοῖς ἀνθρώποις εἰς ἀπόλαυσιν, ἵνα σοι εὐχαριστήσωσιν, ἡμῖν δὲ ἐχαρίσω πνευματικὴν τροφὴν καὶ ποτὸν καὶ ζωὴν αἰώνιον διὰ τοῦ παιδός σου.

10:4 Above all, we thank thee that thou art able to save; to thee be the glory for ever.

10:4 πρὸ πάντων εὐχαριστοῦμέν σοι, ὅτι δυνατὸς εἶ· σοὶ ἡ δόξα εἰς τοὺς αἰῶνας.

10:5 Remember, Lord, thy Church, to redeem it from every evil, and to perfect it in thy love, and gather it together from the four winds,[40] even that which has been sanctified for thy kingdom which thou hast prepared for it; for thine is the kingdom and the glory for ever.

10:5 μνήσθητι, κύριε, τῆς ἐκκλησίας σου, τοῦ ῥύσασθαι αὐτὴν ἐν τῇ ἀγάπῃ σου, καὶ σύναξον αὐτὴν ἀπὸ τῶν τεσσάρων ἀνέμων, τὴν ἁγιασθεῖσαν, εἰς τὴν σὴν βασιλείαν, ἣν ἡτοίμασας αὐτῇ· ὅτι σοῦ ἐστιν ἡ δύναμις καὶ ἡ δόξα εἰς τοὺς αἰῶνας.

10:6 Let grace come, and let this world pass away.[41] Hosanna to the Son of David. If anyone is holy let him come (to the Eucharist); if anyone is not, let him repent. Maranatha.[42] Amen.

---

[40] Matt. 24: 31.
[41] 1 Cor. 7: 31
[42] 1 Cor. 16: 22.

10:6 ἐλθέτω χάρις καὶ παρελθέτω ὁ κόσμος οὗτος. Ὡσαννὰ τῷ θεῷ Δαυείδ. εἴ τις ἅγιός ἐστιν, ἐρχέσθω· εἴ τις οὐκ ἔστι, μετανοείτω· μαρὰν ἀθά· ἀμήν.

10:7 But charge the prophets to give thanks, so far as they are willing to do so.

10:7 τοῖς δὲ προφήταις ἐπιτρέπετε εὐχαριστεῖν ὅσα θέλουσιν.

CHAPTER XI
APOSTLES AND PROPHETS

11:1 Whosoever, therefore, shall come and teach you all these things aforesaid, him do ye receive;

11:1 Ὃς ἂν οὖν ἐλθὼν διδάξῃ ὑμᾶς ταῦτα πάντα τὰ προειρημένα, δέξασθε αὐτόν·

11:2 but if the teacher himself turn and teach another doctrine with a view to subvert you, hearken not to him; but if he come to add to your righteousness, and the knowledge of the Lord, receive him as the Lord.

11:2 ἐὰν δὲ αὐτὸς ὁ διδάσκων στραφεὶς διδάσκῃ ἄλλην διδαχὴν εἰς τὸ καταλῦσαι, μὴ αὐτοῦ ἀκούσητε· εἰς δὲ τὸ προσθεῖναι δικαοσύνην καὶ γνῶσιν κυρίου, δέξασθε αὐτὸν ὡς κύριον.

11:3 But concerning the apostles and prophets, thus do ye according to the doctrine of the Gospel.

11:3 Περὶ δὲ τῶν ἀποστόλων καὶ προφητῶν, κατὰ τὰ δόγμα τοῦ εὐαγγελίου οὕτω ποιήσατε.

11:4 Let every apostle who cometh unto you be received as the Lord.[43]

11:4 πᾶς δὲ ἀπόστολος ἐρχόμενος πρὸς ὑμᾶς δεχθήτω ὡς κύριος·

11:5 He will remain one day, and if it be necessary, a second; but if he remain three days, he is a false prophet.

11:5 οὐ μενεῖ δὲ εἰ μὴ ἡμέραν μίαν· ἐὰν δὲ ᾖ χρεία, καὶ τὴν ἄλλην· τρεῖς δὲ ἐὰν μείνῃ, ψευδοπροφήτης ἐστίν.

11:6 And let the apostle when departing take nothing but bread until he arrive at his resting-place; but if he ask for money, he is a false prophet.

11:6 ἐξερχόμενος δὲ ὁ ἀπόστολος μηδὲν λαμβανέτω εἰ μὴ ἄρτον, ἕως οὗ αὐλισθῇ· ἐὰν δὲ ἀργυριον αἰτῇ, ψευδοπροφήτης ἐστί.

11:7 And ye shall not tempt or dispute with any prophet who speaks in the spirit; for every sin shall be forgiven, but this sin shall not be forgiven.

11:7 Καὶ πάντα προφήτην λαλοῦντα ἐν πνεύματι οὐ πειράσετε οὐδὲ διακρινεῖτε· πᾶσα γὰρ ἁμαρτία ἀφεθήσεται, αὕτη δὲ ἡ ἁμαρτία οὐκ ἀφεθήσεται.

11:8 But not everyone who speaks in the spirit is a prophet, but he is so who hath the disposition of the Lord; by their

---

[43] Matt. 10: 40.

dispositions they therefore shall be known, the false prophet and the prophet.

11:8 οὐ πᾶς δὲ ὁ λαλῶν ἐν πνεύματι προφήτης ἐστίν, ἀλλ' ἐὰν ἔχῃ τοὺς τρόπους κυρίου. ἀπὸ οὖν τῶν τρόπων γνωσθήσεται ὁ ψευδοπροφήτης καὶ ὁ προφήτης.

11:9 And every prophet who orders in the spirit that a table shall be laid, shall not eat of it himself, but if he do otherwise, he is a false prophet;

11:9 καὶ πᾶς προφήτης ὁρίζων τράπεζαν ἐν πνεύματι οὐ φάγεται ἀπ' αὐτῆς, εἰ δὲ μήγε ψευδοπροφήτης ἐστί.

11:10 and every prophet who teaches the truth, if he do not what he teaches is a false prophet;

11:10 πᾶς δὲ προφήτης διδάσκων τὴν ἀλήθειαν, εἰ ἃ διδάσκει οὐ ποιεῖ, ψευδοπρφήτης ἐστί.

11:11 and every prophet who is approved and true, and ministering in the visible mystery of the Church, but who teaches not others to do the things that he does himself, shall not be judged of you, for with God lies his judgment, for in this manner also did the ancient prophets.

11:11 πᾶς δὲ προφήτης δεδοκιμασμένος, ἀληθινός, ποιῶν εἰς μυστήριον κοσμικὸν ἐκκλησίας, μὴ διδάσκων δὲ ποιεῖν, ὅσα αὐτὸς ποιεῖ, οὐ κριθήσεται ἐφ' ὑμῶν· μετὰ θεοῦ γὰρ ἔχει τὴν κρίσιν· ὡσαύτως γὰρ ἐποίησαν καὶ οἱ ἀρχαῖοι προφῆται.

11:12 But whoever shall say in the spirit, Give me money, or things of that kind, listen not to him; but if he tell you

concerning others that are in need that ye should give unto them, let no one judge him.

11:12 ὃς δ᾽ ἂν εἴπῃ ἐν πνεύματι· δός μοι ἀργύρια ἢ ἕτερά τινα, οὐκ ἀκούσεσθε αὐτοῦ· ἐὰν δὲ περὶ ἄλλων ὑστερούντων εἴπῃ δοῦναι, μηδεὶς αὐτὸν κρινέτω.

CHAPTER XII
RECEIVING DISCIPLES

12:1 Let everyone that comes in the name of the Lord be received, but afterwards ye shall examine him and know his character, for ye have knowledge both of good and evil.

12:1 Πᾶς δὲ ὁ ἐρχόμενος ἐν ὀνόματι κυρίου δεχθήτω· ἔπειτα δὲ δοκιμάσαντες αὐτὸν γνώσεσθε, σύνεσιν γὰρ ἕξετε δεξιὰν καὶ ἀριστεράν.

12:2 If the person who comes be a wayfarer, assist him so far as ye are able; but he will not remain with you more than two or three days, unless there be a necessity.

12:2 εἰ μὲν παρόδιός ἐστιν ὁ ἐρχόμενος, βοηθεῖτε αὐτῷ, ὅσον δύνασθε· οὐ μενεῖ δὲ πρὸς ὑμᾶς εἰ μὴ δύο ἢ τρεῖς ἡμέρας, ἐὰν ᾖ ἀνάγκη.

12:3 But if he wishes to settle with you, being a craftsman, let him work, and so eat;

12:3 εἰ δὲ θέλει πρὸς ὑμᾶς καθῆσθαι, τεχνίτης ὤν, ἐργαζέσθω καὶ φαγέτω.

12:4 but if he knows not any craft, provide ye according to you own discretion, that a Christian may not live idle among you;

12:4 εἰ δὲ οὐκ ἔχει τέχνην, κατὰ τὴν σύνεσιν ὑμῶν προνοήσατε, πῶς μὴ ἀργὸς μεθ' ὑμῶν ζήσεται Χριστιανός.

12:5 but if he be not willing to do so, he is a trafficker in Christ. From such keep aloof.

12:5 εἰ δ' οὐ θέλει οὕτω ποιεῖν, χριστέμπορός ἐστι· προσέχετε ἀπὸ τῶν τοιούτων.

CHAPTER XIII
TREATMENT OF PROPHETS

13:1 But every true prophet who is willing to dwell among you is worthy of his meat,

13:1 Πᾶς δὲ προφήτης ἀληθινὸς θέλων καθῆσθαι πρὸς ὑμᾶς ἄξιός ἐστι τῆς τροφῆς αὐτοῦ.

13:2 likewise a true teacher is himself worthy of his meat, even as is a labourer.[44]

13:2 ὡσαύτως διδάσκαλος ἀληθινός ἐστιν ἄξιος καὶ αὐτὸς ὥσπερ ὁ ἐργάτης τῆς τροφῆς αὐτοῦ.

13:3 Thou shalt, therefore, take the firstfruits of every produce of the wine-press and threshing-floor, of oxen and

---

[44] Matt. 10: 10.

sheep, and shalt give it to the prophets, for they are your chief priests;

13:3 πᾶσαν οὖν ἀπαρχὴν γεννημάτων ληνοῦ καὶ ἅλωνος, βοῶν τε καὶ προβάτων λαβὼν δώσεις τὴν ἀπαρχὴν τοῖς προφήταις· αὐτοὶ γάρ εἰσιν οἱ ἀρχιερεῖς ὑμῶν.

13:4 but if ye have not a prophet, give it unto the poor.

13:4 ἐὰν δὲ μὴ ἔχητε προφήτην, δότε τοῖς πτωχοῖς.

13:5 If thou makest a feast, take and give the firstfruits according to the commandment;

13:5 ἐὰν σιτίαν ποιῇς, τὴν ἀπαρχὴν λαβὼν δὸς κατὰ τὴν ἐντολήν.

13:6 in like manner when thou openest a jar of wine or of oil, take the firstfruits and give it to the prophets;

13:6 ὡσαύτως κεράμιον οἴνου ἢ ἐλαίου ἀνοίξας, τὴν ἀπαρχὴν λαβὼν δὸς τοῖς προφήταις·

13:7 take also the firstfruits of money, of clothes, and of every possession, as it shall seem good unto thee, and give it according to the commandment.

13:7 ἀργυρίου δὲ καὶ ἱματισμοῦ καὶ παντὸς κτήματος λαβὼν τὴν ἀπαρχήν, ὡς ἄν σοι δόξῃ, δὸς κατὰ τὴν ἐντολήν.

CHAPTER XIV
THE LORD'S DAY AND THE SACRIFICE

14:1 But on the Lord's Day,[45] **after that ye have assembled together, break bread and give thanks, having in addition confessed your sins,**[46] **that your sacrifice may be pure.**

14:1 Κατὰ κυριακὴν δὲ κυρίου συναχθέντες κλάσατε ἄρτον καὶ εὐχαριστήσατε, προεξομολογησάμενοι τὰ παραπτώματα ὑμῶν, ὅπως καθαρὰ ἡ θυσία ὑμῶν ἡ.

14:2 But let not anyone who hath a quarrel with his companion join with you, until they be reconciled, that your sacrifice may not be polluted,[47]

14:2 πᾶς δὲ ἔχων τὴν ἀμφιβολίαν μετὰ τοῦ ἑταίρου αὐτοῦ μὴ συνελθέτω ὑμῖν, ἕως οὗ διαλλαγῶσιν, ἵνα μὴ κοινωθῇ ἡ θυσία ὑμῶν.

14:3 for it is that which is spoken of by the Lord. In every place and time offer unto me a pure sacrifice, for I am a great King, says the Lord, and my name is wonderful among the Gentiles.[48]

14:3 αὕτη γάρ ἐστιν ἡ ῥηθεῖσα ὑπὸ κυρίου· Ἐν παντὶ τόπῳ καὶ χρόνῳ προσφέρειν μοι θυσίαν καθαράν. ὅτι βασιλεὺς μέγας εἰμί, λέγει κύριος, καὶ τὸ ὄνομά μου θαυμαστὸν ἐν τοῖς ἔθνεσι.

---

[45] Rev. 1: 10.
[46] James 5: 16.
[47] Matt. 5: 23, 24.
[48] Mal. 1: 11, 14.

CHAPTER XV
BISHOPS AND DEACONS

15:1 Elect, therefore, for yourselves bishops and deacons worthy of the Lord, men who are meek and not covetous, and true and approved, for they perform for you the service of prophets and teachers.

15:1 Χειροτονήσατε οὖν ἑαυτοῖς ἐπισκόπους καὶ διακόνους ἀξίους τοῦ κυρίου, ἄνδρας πραεῖς καὶ ἀφιλαργύρους καὶ ἀληθεῖς καὶ δεδοκιμασμένους· ὑμῖν γὰρ λειτουργοῦσι καὶ αὐτοὶ τὴν λειτουργίαν τῶν προφητῶν καὶ διδασκάλων.

15:2 Do not, therefore, despise them, for they are those who are honoured among you, together with the prophets and teachers.

15:2 μὴ οὖν ὑπερίδητε αὐτούς· αὐτοὶ γάρ εἰσιν οἱ τετιμημένοι ὑμῶν μετὰ τῶν προφητῶν καὶ διδασκάλων.

15:3 Rebuke one another, not in wrath but peaceably, as ye have commandment in the Gospel; and, but let no one speak to anyone who walketh disorderly with regard to his neighbour, neither let him be heard by you until he repents.

15:3 Ἐλέγχετε δὲ ἀλλήλους μὴ ἐν ὀργῇ, ἀλλ᾽ ἐν εἰρήνῃ ὡς ἔχετε ἐν τῷ εὐαγγελίῳ· καὶ παντὶ ἀστοχοῦντι κατὰ τοῦ ἑτέρου μηδεὶς λαλείτω μηδὲ παρ᾽ ὑμῶν ἀκουέτω, ἕως οὗ μετανοήσῃ.

15:4 But your prayers and your almsgivings and all your deeds so do, as ye have commandment in the Gospel of our Lord.

15:4 τὰς δὲ εὐχὰς ὑμῶν καὶ τὰς ἐλεημοσύνας καὶ πάσας τὰς πράξεις οὕτω ποιήσατε, ὡς ἔχετε ἐν τῷ εὐαγγελίῳ τοῦ κυρίου ἡμῶν.

CHAPTER XVI
WATCHFULNESS AND THE COMING CHRIST

16:1 Watch concerning your life; let not your lamps be quenched or your loins be loosed,[49] but be ye ready, for ye know not the hour at which our Lord cometh.[50]
16:1 Γρηγορεῖτε ὑπὲρ τῆς ζωῆς ὑμῶν· οἱ λύχνοι ὑμῶν μὴ σβεσθήτωσαν, καὶ αἱ ὀσφύες ὑμῶν μὴ ἐκλυέσθωσαν, ἀλλὰ γίνεσθε ἕτοιμοι· οὐ γὰρ οἴδατε τὴν ὥραν, ἐν ᾗ ὁ κύριος ἡμῶν ἔρχεται.

16:2 But be ye gathered together frequently, seeking what is suitable for your souls; for the whole time of your faith shall profit you not, unless ye be found perfect in the last time.
16:2 πυκνῶς δὲ συναχθήσεσθε ζητοῦντες τὰ ἀνήκοντα ταῖς ψυχαῖς ὑμῶν· οὐ γὰρ ὠφελήσει ὑμᾶς ὁ πᾶς χρόνος τῆς πίστεως ὑμῶν, ἐὰν μὴ ἐν τῷ ἐσχάτῳ καιρῷ τελειωθῆτε.

16:3 For in the last days false prophets and seducers shall be multiplied, and the sheep shall be turned into wolves, and love shall be turned into hate;

---

[49] Luke 12: 35.
[50] Matt. 25: 13.

16:3 ἐν γὰρ ταῖς ἐσχάταις ἡμέραις πληθυνθήσονται οἱ ψευδοπροφῆται καὶ οἱ φθορεῖς, καὶ στραφήσονται τὰ πρόβατα εἰς λύκους, καὶ ἡ ἀγάπη στραφήσεται εἰς μῖσος.

16:4 and because iniquity abounds they shall hate each other, and persecute each other, and deliver each other up; and then shall the Deceiver of the world appear as the Son of God, and shall do signs and wonders,[51] and the earth shall be delivered into his hands; and he shall do unlawful things, such as have never happened since the beginning of the world.

16:4 αὐξανούσης γὰρ τῆς ἀνομίας μισήσουσιν ἀλλήλους καὶ διώξουσι καὶ παραδώσουσι, καὶ τότε φανήσεται ὁ κοσμοπλανὴς ὡς υἱὸσ θεοῦ, καὶ ποιήσει σημεῖα καὶ τέρατα, καὶ ἡ γῆ παραδοθήσεται εἰς χεῖρας αὐτοῦ, καὶ ποιήσει ἀθέμιτα, ἃ οὐδέποτε γέγονεν ἐξ αἰῶνος.

16:5 Then shall the creation of man come to the fiery trial of proof, and many shall be offended and shall perish; but they who remain in their faith shall be saved by the rock of offence itself.

16:5 τότε ἥξει ἡ κτίσις τῶν ἀνθρώπων εἰς τὴν πύρωσιν τῆς δοκιμασίας, καὶ σκανδαλισθήσονται πολλοὶ καὶ ἀπολοῦνται, οἱ δὲ ὑπομείναντες ἐν τῇ πίστει αὐτῶν σωθήσονται ὑπ' αὐτου τοῦ καταθέματος.

---

[51] Matt. 24: 24.

16:6 And then shall appear the signs of the truth; first the sign of the appearance in heaven, then the sign of the sound of the trumpet, and thirdly the resurrection of the dead

16:6 καὶ τότε φανήσεται τὰ σημεῖα τῆς ἀληθείας· πρῶτον σημεῖον ἐκπετάσεως ἐν οὐρανῷ, εἶτα σημεῖον φωνῆς σάπιγγος, καὶ τὸ τρίτον ἀνάστασις νεκρῶν.

16:7 not of all, but as it has been said, The Lord shall come and all his saints with him;[52]

16:7 οὐ πάντων δέ, ἀλλ᾽ ὡς ἐρρέθη· Ἥξει ὁ κύριος καὶ πάντες οἱ ἅγιοι μετ᾽ αὐτοῦ.

16:8 then shall the world behold the Lord coming on the clouds of heaven.

16:8 τότε ὄψεται ὁ κόσμος τὸν κύριον ἐρχόμενον ἐπάνω τῶν νεφελῶν τοῦ οὐρανοῦ.

---

[52] Matt. 24: 30.

GOD BE WITH YOU

Made in the USA
Middletown, DE
14 October 2024

62602649R00027